Small Group
Essentials

**KEYS TO UNLOCK
YOUR GROUP'S
POTENTIAL**

CWR
Andy Peck

Contents

Introduction

In broad terms, a small group is a group of people (typically 6–16) who intentionally gather together to further God's purposes in some way. Many churches run what I call 'classic small groups', which meet to connect with one another by praying and studying the Bible together, amongst other things. Other groups meet around a shared activity, aimed at developing connections and welcoming people from outside the church. I would also include under this definition groups that meet with the aim of mastering a topic or area of the faith over a set period, such as parenting skills, debt recovery, investigating Christianity (eg Alpha and Christianity Explored). These typically have a small group element, albeit with taught material as well. This book focuses on small groups run under the auspices of a local church, but much of the material would equally apply to a charity running small groups, such as those serving young people or in the workplace.

My own experience of small groups is widely varied. I attended a small group as a student, and I later went on to train students in small group leadership as a Universities and Colleges Christian Fellowship staff worker. I have been part of a small group in all the churches I have attended, including while serving as a pastor and charity worker. I used to lead a small group with my wife in our present church, and teach on small group leadership at Waverley Abbey House for CWR. I have known both struggle and success in small group leadership and I draw upon these ups and downs in this book.

If we are honest, there are pitfalls of small group leadership. In many cases, the impetus that launched a small group can be slow, leaving a group that is simply going through the motions.

You may have picked up this book because you feel your group has become a little stale. Or you may be happy with your small group and simply want to enhance it in some way. Whatever your motivation, I hope you will find this book a stimulus to your thinking and prayers.

There will be many opportunities for you to reflect on your group and to look to the future. You may want to read the book with a group co-leader so that you can reflect and plan together. After the first three chapters, the order in which you read this book is not vital, so feel free to head to the parts that especially interest you. My prayer is that this book might serve as a tool to help you unlock your group's potential, and kindle a fresh openness to what God can and will do.

01: Consider your potential

Small groups have amazing potential to nurture people in their Christian faith. And just as we are all a 'work in progress' as individuals, small groups themselves often have some distance to go before they are realising their potential. Before you can move forward, it is essential to know where you are right now as a small group. Consider the following 'What?' 'Why?' and 'How?' questions. They are mostly fact-based and will help you gather an overview of your group.

What?

Take some time to answer the following questions, which are all to do with *what* your group is exactly. Later, you will be encouraged to consider whether any changes could be made, but for now, this is simply to record the current shape of your group.

Who is your small group for primarily (men, women, mixed, age range, level of maturity)?

How often do you meet?

_____

_____

Where do you meet?

_____

_____

What time of day do you meet?

_____

_____

How long does a meeting typically last?

_____

_____

How many are in your group?

_____

_____

Does attendance fluctuate or is it steady?

_____

_____

Now, getting a little more specific, let's look at four core aspects of a classic small group. Ask yourself the following questions. (If some do not apply to your group, move on to the next.) If you like, jot down your reflections in the space provided.

Bible study

- Do people seem to be responsive to what God says through His Word?
- Is the level of study appropriate for everyone?
- Is there a good level of engagement, discussion and even healthy disagreement?

_____

_____

_____

_____

_____

Fellowship

- Are people sharing their genuine needs?
- Is care being shown for individuals spontaneously?
- Are people meeting socially outside the group?

_____

_____

_____

_____

_____

Witness

- Do group members share testimonies of discussing Jesus with colleagues, family or strangers?
- Are you praying as a group for those who do not yet know Jesus?
- Are there opportunities for members to invite these people to church services or activities?

_____

_____

_____

_____

_____

Prayer

- Does everyone feel welcome to pray out loud?
- Do you see and rejoice in answers to prayer?
- Have you observed or heard of growth in anyone's prayer life?

_____

_____

_____

_____

_____

Finally, what words would you use to describe your group?

(Tick any that apply)

○ Enthusiastic   ○ Focused

○ Committed   ○ Directionless

○ Apathetic   ○ Studious

○ Quiet   ○ Friendly

○ Loud   ○ Fun

Other _____

Why?

Perhaps you have never considered the exact reason why your group meets before. Even if it has never been stated, there is most likely an underlying reason why you meet. It's important to be aware of this because it will help you to be more intentional and focused. And if you stray from your purpose, you can either re-evaluate the purpose itself or bring your group back in line with your objectives.

What are the current purposes of your group?

(Tick any that apply)

○ Study the Bible

○ Care for one another

○ Connect with other believers

○ Pray for those in the group

○ Pray for specific situations or an area of the world

○ Provide opportunity for non-believers to discover Jesus

○ Understand a topic

○ Train in an area of Christian ministry

○ Provide support for others serving in an area of ministry

○ Nurture a believer in a particular stage of faith

○ Provide an opportunity to discuss doubts
○ Support those with physical or mental health challenges
○ Enjoy a shared activity

Other _____

How?

This leads us on to the questions of 'How?' It's helpful to question how we can fulfil certain purposes of our group. Looking at the purposes you ticked or wrote down, try to think of practical ways in which you facilitate these. For example, if you ticked 'Care for one another', do you make time to go around the group and ask how everyone is doing? Do you encourage people to talk in twos or threes so they can share openly? Do you lead by example by texting others during the week to see how they are, or provide practical help outside the group meeting?

_____

_____

_____

_____

_____

_____

_____

_____

_____

Evaluate your 'work in progress'

Once you have written down as much as you think is helpful, go back through this chapter and highlight any answers or thoughts that you could see room for improvement. You could use this space to write your initial thoughts.

_____

_____

_____

_____

_____

_____

_____

_____

_____

_____

_____

_____

Now that you have considered your small group in more depth, you are in great stead to explore more keys to unlocking your group's potential. You may want to return to this chapter now and again to review your answers and reflections.

02: Develop a compelling vision

Take the following four churches...

In one Midlands-based church, small groups have been going for a number of years and involve around 50% of the 150-member church. Some of the groups study the material from the previous Sunday sermon and some do their own thing. Unfortunately, the groups are not reaching the younger people who find the format uninteresting. A number of people in their twenties no longer attend their group as they did not see the purpose.

In a smaller church on the south coast, the small groups function and provide some support for the members, but the studies are generally hit and miss. People keep attending because small group attendance is a high value in the church, but when there's a good excuse not to be there, many will take it. Group leaders have been leading for a long time and many would love to hand the responsibility on to a new leader, if only they could find a good reason for doing so.

A London-based church has seen some significant growth in recent years through outreach programmes and projects serving those impoverished or seeking asylum in the UK. But they have not been so successful when it comes to integrating those who have come to faith through a small group.

A busy, commuter-based church has few willing or mature enough to take on small group leadership even though there are enough church members for at least eight groups. For the moment, they are hoping that the Sunday services will meet their needs.

What do all these churches have in common? They are all in need of vision for their small groups. When thinking about the vision for our individual group, we need to reflect on the vision of the wider church. Then we can explore how our vision and aims fit with what the church is doing and God's purposes for His people.

Our church's vision

Plenty of good things will happen in a church without clear strategic planning. But if a church has not decided collectively on how they believe God is leading them, vital areas may be forgotten or overlooked. Churches, charities and businesses create vision statements and mission statements to clarify how they want to operate and what they want to aim for. There is no precise rule about what these statements should include, but a simple formula is to think through:

- Why do we exist as a church?
- Where are we heading as a church?
- How are we going to get there?

Why do we exist as a church?

Very helpfully, Scripture answers this question for us. By definition, a church is a gathering of people who have acknowledged that Jesus is Lord of all, and seek to live their life according to that truth.

The word 'church' in our English Bibles comes from the Greek word *ekklesia*, which essentially means 'an assembly of people called together'. As such, 'church' is an assembly of Christians 'called' by God to be followers of Jesus. So, take away all the accoutrements of church that have become add-ons over the centuries, and this lies the heart of why we exist. Gathering together. Discipleship. Growth.

The New Testament describes the kinds of things that believers did to fulfil this:

- Worship of God (1 Pet. 2:9)
- Teaching of the Word of God (Col. 3:16; 2 Tim. 2:2)
- Spending time together so that we may love one another (John 13:34; Gal. 6:10)
- Celebration of communion (1 Cor. 11:26)
- Reaching those outside the Church in word and deed (Matt. 28:18–20; Acts 4:29; 8:4; 2 Tim. 4:1,2)
- Helping believers remain true to Christ (Matt. 18:15–17; Titus 3:10)

Most churches include these kinds of activities somewhere in their week, and all can be done both within a larger gathering and in smaller groups.

Every church does what they do for a reason, even if that reason does not feel chosen. It may be a case of 'we have always done it this way' or 'these are the practices of churches like us' (often regarding a denominational affiliation) or 'this is the vision of a former leader that we respected and have carried on'.

Church history is the story of Christ followers who sought to align their beliefs with their practice. We could make arguments for certain practices to be priorities, but at least we can agree on the key reason why we exist: to gather to bring glory to God.

Where are we heading as a church?

Many churches find it helpful to have a vision statement: a succinct, one-sentence statement encompassing all they want to achieve as a company of God's people. It is based on why they exist, but seeks to bring a dynamism to what they aim to be about, describing the goal they wish to reach. Here are some examples of a church vision statement:

- We will become a movement of disciple-making disciples.
- We will grow to be a vibrant church of many more followers of Jesus.
- We will become a God-raised, Spirit-filled army for the twenty-first century – convinced of our calling, moving forward together.
- We will be a family, rooted in the Word of God and prayer, whose love for Christ and for one another overflows in joyful sharing of the gospel with all.

How are we going to get there?

A mission statement specifies the steps your church will take to achieve the vision statement. It may even include a timeframe. It can be helpful for a church to have two missions: an internal mission, for how it intends to help believers; and an external mission, for what it intends to do in its work in the wider world.

If your vision statement is: 'We will grow to be a vibrant church of many more followers of Jesus', your mission statement might be the following:

- We will have regular events that aim to serve non-believers.
- We will invest in courses designed to help Christians mature in their faith.

- We will encourage church members to spend time connecting with people outside the church.
- Our members will know their spiritual gifts and will be given opportunities to use them.

Vision statements and mission statements do need to be written prayerfully. We also need to have an awareness of when they may need adjusting because of things happening in the community or what God is doing in the life of the church. The future will include things we cannot anticipate: community changes affecting members, a ministry that takes off when people come to faith, changes in economic policy that influences the community (eg when austerity measures in the UK led to a rise in the take up of food banks). So, it is wise to revisit your mission statement in the light of events such as these.

In my experience, many churches restrict their statements to what the church organises corporately, perhaps forgetting that the church is made up of individuals. Part of the church may commute to other communities, fly overseas, be in schools, colleges and universities, serve in shops, run local businesses etc. Perhaps we should consider these aspects as well?

So, does your church have a vision statement and mission statement? If yes, fill them in below. If not yet, could you speak to your church leadership about the need for a vision? And for now, could you write what you perceive to be the current vision and mission?

Our church's vision statement:

_____

_____

_____

_____

_____

_____

Our church's mission statement:

_____

_____

_____

_____

_____

_____

Our small group's vision

Now that you have considered your church's vision and mission – the wider picture – take time to focus in on your small group, asking those same questions.

Why do we exist as a small group?

In some churches, small groups are so intimately connected to the mission as the means of fulfilling the vision that their role becomes very clear. When church leaders have been asked why small groups exist in their church, the answers typically include language about spiritual growth. They may include phrases such as 'to make disciples', 'to help members grow in Christ', 'to become fully devoted followers of Jesus', 'to become all that God intends' and so on. These are commendable aims, which respond to Jesus' Great Commission to 'go and make disciples of all nations' (Matt. 28:19).

So perhaps small groups exist to facilitate personal growth in ways the corporate church cannot. Take the command to love one another. Loving one another is simply seeking another's good. If you attend a weekly service of worship with, say, four-hundred other people – you sing the same songs, listen to the same message, put money in the same collection – you do not necessarily connect with anyone at a level that would enable you to give and receive love in the biblical sense. If you are to love, you need to get to know people, and a small group is a great way of doing that. It's not the only way of course, and small groups can do many other things, but for a newcomer to a large church, looking to follow Christ in this matter, small groups fit the bill.

Many of the commands of the New Testament assumes a degree of relationship within the body that can make the commands and blessings of community life real. Most of the 'one another's of the New Testament, such as 'encourage one another', 'accept one another' and so on (there are over forty!) assume a smaller gathering where such an outcome can be meaningful.

The apostle Peter speaks of a sort of personal progression, which may help us consider the reason why we exist as a small group: 'For this very reason, make every effort to add to your faith goodness; and to goodness, knowledge; and to knowledge, self-control; and to self-control, perseverance; and to perseverance, godliness; and to godliness, mutual affection; and to mutual affection, love. For if you possess these qualities in increasing measure, they will keep you from being ineffective and unproductive in your knowledge of our Lord Jesus Christ' (2 Pet. 1:5–9).

Where are we heading as a small group?

In the light of the church's vision and mission and the factors considered in this chapter, write your first draft of a compelling vision. It should excite you in some way. Feel free to return and amend it as you work through this book.

Our small group's vision statement:

_____

_____

_____

_____

_____

_____

How are we going to get there?

There are very few imperatives when it comes to small groups. We cannot say, 'thou shalt have small groups that will meet for 90 minutes on the third day of the week'! Scripture does not prescribe the size or scope for a successful small group.

The important thing to remember is that your compelling vision will need to encompass a desire for a future that is possible. In his book *Seven Habits of Highly Effective People*, Stephen Covey urges readers to spend their time on the areas where they have influence and not on areas of mere concern that they can do nothing about. You may drive yourself crazy if you fail to distinguish between the two.

Another important area of discernment is knowing how to change the right things. You may have heard the parable of the lifeboat station. It goes something like this...

Concerned inhabitants of a small coastal town began a lifeboat station to save those in trouble at sea. It was just one hut with a lifeboat and a few dedicated souls who kept an eye out for anyone in trouble. Over time, its prowess grew – what had been just a lifeboat station became something of a club. Other non-lifeboat activities went on, which attracted a number of people who loved the fellowship but had little interest in the lifesaving elements of the station. The simple hut was replaced by a larger building, serving meals and taking care of the needs of the club members. As years passed, fewer people with concerns for lifesaving were part of the club at all, and eventually the club opted to dispense with the upkeep of the boats, which was draining the resources its members preferred to use for other things. The club was far grander than the hut, but its capacity to fulfil its original purpose was completely gone.

Make sure you want to change your group for the right reasons. I have met small group leaders who are worried their groups have too many heated discussions, but perhaps this is a good sign that people care. I have heard some say that their groups are not 'deep enough', but perhaps this is a perception issue. I have met small group leaders who are disgruntled by members who are 'too quiet', but perhaps in reality these members were recovering from a tough season in life and did not trust themselves to share, perhaps because their emotions were still close to the surface.

When it comes to considering improvements to small groups, let us make sure we are concerned with what concerns God and not the peripheral matters which may concern us.

So, using your vision statement, try writing a mission statement below. These are the steps you need to take to fulfil your vision. Again, you can return to this again later. To help, you could consider the following areas:

- Personnel – Who will lead? How will you develop leaders?
- Focus – Who is the group for? What will the group accomplish?
- Communication – How will you share the vision?
- Time frame – When will all this happen?
- Resources – What materials will you use? How much will it cost?
- Development – What are the stages of development you envisage?

Our small group's mission statement:

_____

_____

_____

_____

_____

_____

03: Use your group for growth

You may be aware that church attendance in the UK is reportedly declining. Surveys and research during the past few decades constituently show that about two thirds of people in the UK claim to have no connection with any religion or church. Although decline has largely continued in recent years, the trend is bucked in independent, new, Orthodox, and Pentecostal churches, as well as in smaller, non-traditional churches, many of which report growth in attendance. Of course, church attendance is just one measure of faith, but let us not ignore the facts. So, what can we do?

How about using small groups?

Small groups. Evangelism. Really?

Consider that, in the past and present, small groups have been a powerful catalyst for growth. Many major revivals have been started by small groups of believers with ready access to the Bible.

How could the 12 disciples possibly have taken care of 3,000 new converts? Chances are that these disciples used the lessons learned by Jesus to disciple these new believers. We read in Acts 2:46-47: 'Every day they continued to meet together in the temple courts. They broke bread in their homes and ate together with glad and sincere hearts, praising God and enjoying the favour of all the people. And the Lord added to their number daily those who were being saved'. Later, in Acts 20:20, the apostle Paul reminds the members of the church at Ephesus that he taught them publicly and from house to house.

The letter that Paul wrote to the Christians in Rome was written to believers who met in people's homes. In his letter, Paul indicates that one of these groups met in the home of Priscilla and Aquila: 'Greet Priscilla and Aquila, my co-workers in Christ Jesus. They risked their lives for me. Not only I but all the churches of the Gentiles are grateful to them. Greet also the church that meets at their house' (Rom. 16:3–5).

In eighteenth-century Britain, a spiritual awakening came when John Wesley and Charles Whitefield's preaching led many to faith and brought spiritual renewal to the then declining Anglican Church. Wesley in particular formed small groups, known as 'classes'. They were places where people were nurtured in their faith and enabled to reach out to their friends and colleagues.

One of the largest churches in the world grew through small groups. Pastor Dr David Yonggi Cho believes that the small group is the best method of evangelism because it becomes the centre of where life happens in its local area. Cho trained his leaders to be sensitive to the needs of others so that they can minister to those needs and then invite those individuals to the small group, where they may encounter Jesus Christ.

Closer to home, perhaps, are the Alpha groups. The foundation of these is small group discussions that enable seekers to reflect on the talks in a relaxed and non-pressured environment. To date, over 29 million people from 169 different countries have been to an Alpha course.

Small groups. Evangelism. Worth considering!

Are we ready?

It is often said, when someone suggests their group should engage with evangelism, 'Are we ready? Don't we need to grow spiritually first in order to evangelise?'

The comment is well meant and has some truth. We do need to know 'the way' before we start pointing it out to others. But it also suggests that there is a moment in a Christian's life when they graduate from small group Bible study, at last mature and able to evangelise, as if there is no 'maturing' taking place as the believer witnesses to friends. Thankfully, as we see in the Gospels, Andrew did not wait to complete six months of intensive study before grabbing his brother Peter and saying, 'We have found the Messiah' (John 1:40–42).

We all need a place to grow spiritually, but let us not allow the fear that we will not grow put us off involvement in a small group that has an evangelistic aim. Indeed, it could be the making of us.

Three ways that small groups can stimulate growth

1. Courses

There are off-the-shelf courses that employ small group discussions, such as Alpha, Christianity Explored, The Y-Course and The Life Course. In many churches, these sorts of courses are the most common means by which people become Christians. They all include accessible teaching, exploratory questions and suggested time for discussion. This is just one way, however, and does not need to be the only way of encouraging evangelism and growth.

2. Bible studies

There are also approaches that use a more classic Bible study technique. Rebecca Manley Pippert, who famously said that evangelism was not something you would do to your dog let alone your best friend, developed a simple approach of reading the Bible with the students she was aiming to serve in Spain. The text would raise the questions, and she would simply help them grasp what it was saying. Her approach to her friends was, 'What have you got to lose?' Her approach is outlined in her bestselling book, *Out of the Saltshaker and into the World* (IVP, 2010).

Some years ago I met a man who employed this approach to plant churches in Austria. We were at a student conference together and I noticed a thick-set man with a large moustache across the room, clearly on his own. I introduced myself, asking what he did as we sat down for lunch. His reply was totally unexpected.

'I go sailing and skiing with non-Christians.'

In my mind I was wondering what mission he worked for and how I could sign up.

'Really? Tell me more.'

'I am an American missionary in Austria, a predominantly Catholic country, but with lots of scepticism about Christianity. I am an American in their country and so when I get talking to people they naturally ask why I am there. And I don't tell them.'

This was the strangest missionary I had ever met.

He continued, 'I am playful and will eventually say, "I am here to learn German, but if you want to know about my main work, read the Gospel of John with me." They start reading and if they have questions, I simply say "keep reading", as my German was not good enough to respond with anything else, at least not in the early months. I was praying that the Holy Spirit would teach them.'

It clearly works. He had planted one church and was on to his second when I met him. He told me that, as a general rule, they would come to faith by John chapter 7!

The missionary in question was Floyd Schneider, and his book, *Evangelism for the Fainthearted* (Kregel Publications, 1999) explores the approach in more detail.

An advanced version of this approach is the Discovery Bible Study – a type of small group that is bearing incredible fruit in various parts of the world: both the so-called developed and developing world, including the USA.

The idea is that you study the Bible with non-believers, and as you read the passage you ask the following questions:

• What does this teach us about God?
• What does this teach us about the human condition?
• What is one concrete action that I can do this week to demonstrate obedience to what I've learned?
• Who does God want me to share this truth with this week?

These might sound like typical questions for a small group made up of Christians. The genius of the approach is that you make sure that the majority of the group are non-believers and simply ask them to join in as much as possible. You do not ask them to sign up to any creedal beliefs, or even to accept that the Bible is the Word of God, at least not at this stage. Of course, you would need a few things to be in place, such as a genuine connection with non-believers that would lead someone to be interested, a willingness to read and think about a topic in this way (it is not everyone's cup of tea), and an understanding of the need to facilitate discussion without attempts to 'evangelise' too early.

Your concern is that those in the group will meet with God and want to follow Him. But that process can take time and will be their response to the Holy Spirit. Your job is not to force the issue, but to allow them the space to think about and discuss the passage. The beauty is that this approach is so successful that once it is up and running, the attendees tend to do the 'recruiting' for you.

3. Supporting one another

Maybe you think the prospect of gathering non-believers to read the Bible is pretty remote. Why not use a small group as a training and support group to equip believers to understand their faith with a view to sharing it? This can include many kinds of witness, from what is sometimes called 'gossiping the gospel' through to answering questions, and (if done well, with the right training) even door-to-door, open air approaches.

In the UK, we face an increasingly hostile environment, buoyed by the sometimes negative view of the media, widespread ignorance of the truth of the Gospel, and an increasingly multi-faith nation where claims that our faith is *the* faith appear arrogant. The Church's stance on marriage and sexuality appears out of step. Christians are seen as those who hold views at odds with mainstream society. There is plenty of reason why gathering Christians within this context to understand their faith better could be a vital way for a church to turn decline into growth.

J. John's *The Natural Evangelism Course* (Philo Trust, 2014) is a great tool if you are looking for material on which to base your approach.

Evaluate your small group

Consider that churches operate with a 'come and see' or a 'go and tell' approach.

'Come and see' churches have a range of activities that may present the gospel in jargon-free ways, or are completely neutral for non-believers to connect with those in the church – such as parents and toddlers, sports groups, arts and crafts, or meal-based groups. Their church services may be aimed at non-believers alongside the believers who attend.

'Go and tell' churches major on building up believers in order that they may have a robust faith and be able to stand for Christ, and share Him in the places where they live, work and play. Hence, they may have relatively few corporate evangelistic activities. They may perceive 'come and see' churches as 'events driven' and say that they fail to encourage members to engage in the world.

As strategies to reach people, both have merit. The key question is whether your strategy is enabling people who are not yet Christians to hear and respond to the gospel. To give yourself an indication of this, try to answer the following questions, reflecting on the last year perhaps.

How many non-believers have attended your group?

_____

Have many people have come to faith in your group?

_____

Are members of your group having meaningful contact with people outside the church?

_____

Have members of your group brought others outside the group to faith?

_____

Are many of your meetings designed to help believers share their faith?

_____

Are many of your meetings designed to help non-believers discover faith?

_____

Are your group members confident they can bring non-believers to church?

_____

Considering your answers, in what ways would you like to improve your group? Remember, we can only change what is in our line of influence.

_____

_____

_____

Moving forward

If you decide that you want to use your small group for evangelistic purposes, here are a few pointers.

Identify those already making connections with people outside of the church

This should ideally include everyone, but you will know those who seem to have a special capacity for this. These are the people who speak without jargon, who connect with non-believers (whatever the cultural nuance is) and who can help them ease into a suitable small group.

Pray that God will show you what to try and what to avoid

Just because Alpha 'works' does not necessarily mean it is right for your group. But are there ways of evangelising that you have not considered before reading this chapter, which you may now try? Ask God to give you wisdom and discernment in this.

Have a 'pilot' mentality

Do not be afraid to try a method out. If you make it clear to your group that you are piloting the idea, then people know that it may or may not work, and that it is OK if it does not. There will be a chance to tweak and refine it in light of feedback. Here are some further ideas to help spark your own:

- Start a group outreach in a local nursing home, where a church member already visits
- Start a Bible study for parents who meet to drop off children at school
- Run an Alpha group specifically for young people

- Have someone gifted in evangelism lead a few 'training sessions' in the group

Allow things to develop as naturally as possible

Strike a balance between being proactive and motivational but not too forceful. Every group of believers has its own DNA and nuances, which the Holy Spirit will take and use, so trust Him to lead you.

So, in what ways could you use your small group for growth? Which of the ideas and approaches listed in this chapter interest you the most? If you like, jot down your thoughts here.

_____

_____

_____

_____

_____

_____

_____

If you want to change or add to the vision for your small group in the light of this chapter, or if you want to make any changes to the mission statement, revisit the end of Chapter 2 and update them.

04: Value leadership

Small groups need leading, and there are all kinds of approaches to fulfilling this role. Your ultimate job as the leader, or co-leader, is to keep the group on track, focused on the real reason for gathering and sidestepping the lesser goals that may distract.

Some groups share the leading of the meetings and group studies. But even in these groups, there is generally a leader who provides an ongoing facilitating and guiding presence. They are then able to evaluate what is happening and pray for God to work in and through the group's activities.

The fact that a group is 'led' means that it is not a group of people who merely gather together to share fellowship and see what happens. In the first two chapters, you considered why your group meets, and then you looked to develop a compelling vision. There is a purpose for gathering, and you as the leader can champion this. In this chapter, we will consider how we can value our leadership roles by developing certain qualities.

So what is required of us as leaders? All churches can have different approaches. Rick Warren, Senior Pastor of Saddleback Community Church, California, once related how he was praying about the small groups at the church. He was asking God how he could increase the number of groups and was wondering about whether he could double them, when he sensed God say, 'What about if they increased by ten times?' He was stunned by this, but then set about thinking. He concluded that if they changed the requirements of the leaders, then they might be able to get close. At that point, the church only selected people with strong pastoral qualities and a high knowledge of the Bible. He knew that this kind of leader was in short supply. Warren decided to provide some Bible teaching and discussion questions, recorded on a DVD, that would form the 'teaching component' of all the small groups. All that he required of the small group leaders was that they were hospitable, had a suitably sized place to meet and a DVD player! When he announced this change to the congregation they had a flood of interest. Suddenly, increasing the small groups tenfold was not so daft. The church today averages 25,000 in attendance (the size of a reasonably sized British town!).

I'm not suggesting that all churches apply this method to their groups. Rather, this simply illustrates how we may be limiting the amount of groups we could run by making our requirements too great. I have seen churches that require leaders to attend six months of weekly training before they can lead a group. If there is the capacity to train people in this kind of intensity, then perhaps it is best, but we can all consider whether our requirements are realistic and helpful, or whether they are onerous and dissuading.

So where do we start when thinking about the really key qualities needed in a leader? Later in this chapter, we will consider the kinds of qualities leaders of different kinds of groups might need. But first, here are some general principles that we can apply to all.

Key qualities of a leader

The apostle Paul advised his young friends Timothy and Titus of the qualities required of the leaders (elders) of the churches in Ephesus and Crete (1 Tim. 3:1–7; Titus 1:5–9). Today, these are qualities traditionally looked for in those serving as a minister, vicar, pastor, lay-elder or lay-deacon in a local church, but can be instructive for us as small group leaders as well.

By and large, they are the kind of qualities developed in a follower of Jesus who gives due attention to how they are living with others. They are illustrative of the kind of person who has grown in Christ to the point where this kind of character is 'second nature'. Put simply, a good leader is:

- Above reproach; blameless
- Faithful to their spouse
- Temperate, not given to drunkenness
- Self-controlled
- Respectable
- Hospitable
- Able to teach sound doctrine
- Not violent but gentle
- Not quarrelsome
- Not a lover of money
- Not pursuing dishonest gain
- Managing their family well

Paul also says a leader should not be a recent convert (literally someone 'newly planted'), suggesting that someone might need to have continued following Jesus for a few years and weathered the storms of faith and life.

The verse on being able to manage the family might be perplexing for someone keen to serve as a leader, whose children have not begun to follow Christ or have gone their own way. We need to interpret the Bible from that context into our own before looking for application. I think it simply means that if there are big battles within the home, it may be an indication that an underlying problem needs addressing before the person is able to lead. But it would be wrong to use this as a law prohibiting anyone ever leading if they have a child who has drifted away from faith, at whatever age.

The capacity to teach is not typically required in a small group context. Indeed a 'teacher' type might not be ideal in a discussion-based study. But groups need those with a good biblical knowledge and ability to discern how truth should be applied.

To add a few more helpful thoughts to Paul's list of qualities, I would like to consider how leadership has a strong influencing component.

Influence comes through a combination of example and speech. Many leaders are not conscious of the way they lead but it is clear that they do. I have known people who have not necessarily been strong speakers, or 'personalities', but so exude a walk with God that people follow them. So I would add that a good leader will have:

- A desire to see Christians grow in their faith
- The ability to speak warmly and confidently
- The capacity to call people to action (sometimes depending on the kind of group)
- The ability to articulate clearly what the group is about
- The ability to listen and discern the group's mood and needs
- The ability to lead discussions
- The perseverance to stick with leading, irrespective of how it seems to be going

- The time to give to a regular gathering

Other desirable (but not essential) skills and qualities include:
- Good time management
- Organisational qualities (or a spouse or close friend who can help)
- A sense of humour
- The capacity to connect people with one another
- The ownership of a decent coffee machine (just joking! But a sense of hospitality, even when it is not in your own home, is important)

There is also an aspect of pastoral care involved in small group leadership. (When I have led pastoral care courses, I always enjoy the attendees' smiles when I say that it helps if pastoral carers like people!) A top quality in a leader is the ability to connect with a wide range of people and seek others' growth.

The word 'pastoral' covers a broad range of activities and can be an intimidating word. A small group leader might compare their capacity to offer pastoral care with that of a pastoral worker or 'ordained' leader. What can be forgotten is that much pastoral care is incumbent upon every member of a church, not just those deputed to be leaders. We are called to practice the 'one another's of the New Testament. There are 44 in total and they are all addressed to gatherings of believers, not just the leaders. Here are a few:
- Love one another (Rom. 13:8)
- Honour one another above yourselves (Rom. 12:10)
- Live in harmony with one another (Rom. 12:16)
- Stop passing judgment on one another (Rom. 14:13)
- Accept one another, just as Christ accepted you (Rom. 15:7)

- Instruct one another (Rom. 15:4)
- Forgive one another (Col. 3:13)

As small group leaders, pastoral care of group members could include:
- Practical help at times of crisis
- Chatting about issues
- Mentoring
- Regular contact with members

There is a legitimate concern with pastoral care. Some issues or situations may be beyond our knowledge or expertise. It may be that a situation will stretch you, your faith and your trust in God. There are plenty of believers who have felt out of their depth, only to see God step in. But it may indeed be the case that some form of specialist help is wise, such as from a counsellor or pastor.

Leading other kinds of small groups

So far, our discussion of small groups has assumed a 'classic' small group involving Bible study, prayer and the sharing of life that comes with it. But there are many other kinds of group to consider. The above qualities may be adjusted when a different kind of group is in question.

Shared activity groups
A small group that meets primarily for fellowship around a shared activity, with an openness to people outside the faith, should ideally have some more mature believers and especially some with an eye for connecting with non-believers. But the leader

(or organiser) does not necessarily need all the qualities that the classic small group leader needs. For example, you might be a relatively new believer. Your strength might then be that you have a group of non-believing friends whom you can bring into the church's orbit through a non-threatening, shared activity.

Life improvement groups

A group that is focused on helping people to learn a topic or work through a life situation should ideally be led by someone with life experience. For example, a parenting group should be led by parents. Although, it may be that someone leads a group without any direct experience but has good knowledge of the subject, such as those leading groups looking to help those divorced, or in debt, or facing addiction. These leaders will need to work hard to ensure that the content is not too theoretical.

Teaching-based groups

For a group that is investigating Christianity and intending spiritual growth, the leader or team of leaders needs to have some Bible knowledge and ability to teach. This is true even if the group is using a DVD, as subsequent discussion still requires someone who has knowledge and wisdom about the faith.

Service-based groups

Some small groups have service as their purpose. Perhaps they meet to clean, lead worship, or run the coffee bar. These groups may also function as a way of members supporting one another's lives, and so the leader will also need to have some of the qualities of a classic small group leader.

Mentoring and coaching groups

Mentoring and coaching is typically a one-to-one activity, but there are occasions where groups of people are mentored or coached. Mentoring can be defined as the imparting of skills and approaches within a field of expertise. Hence groups might meet to be mentored in areas such as worship leading and preaching over a period of time. In this kind of group, the leader needs to be competent in the field in which they are mentoring. Coaching can be defined as the facilitating of growth in another by using listening and questions. The coach does not need competence in the field necessarily but competence as a coach.

Reflect on your leadership qualities

Considering all of the qualities and responsibilities we have explored, think about which ones you particularly display well. Write down these, along with qualities you would like to develop further. If you are unsure, ask a person, who knows you well, which qualities they see in you (we tend to underplay our strengths).

_____

_____

_____

_____

_____

_____

_____

05: Seek God's involvement

It perhaps goes without saying that your small group needs God. You need God's presence as you meet. You need His inspiration in what you do (in planning and execution), and as you read His Word.

The issue with assuming that 'it goes without saying' is that we can become complacent and forget to 'say' or indeed 'ask' God for His presence, or look to see what He is doing.

It is worth reminding yourself that God is keen to be with you in your group. He does not have small group favourites! He is love, and longs to take us on and bless us richly. God is the most thrilling and exciting factor of your small group. As such, in working to reach your purpose and vision, your dependency needs to be on Him.

God is 'omnipresent', meaning everywhere. There is nowhere in this whole universe where He cannot be. He chooses to manifest His presence at certain places and for His own purposes. We can seek this but not control it. If you and I are aware of His manifest presence we will know it, and this can lead to a variety of reactions on our part, including crying, laughter, shaking, a sense of peace, a sense of joy. Most would say these kinds of overwhelming reactions are rare, depending on the church and its expectation.

In parallel with this, the Holy Spirit lives within those who follow Him. Our consciousness of His presence will vary. We grieve Him when we sin, and can quench His work when we do not allow Him to work. God can of course override our wills, but He can choose to not go where He is not invited.

It is therefore worth acknowledging that your small group can hinder God's work. It can be merely a pleasant time of human interaction, but fail to touch people's lives.

God's involvement in our individual lives

The individuals in your group will be at different stages in their walk with God. As the group leader, you seek to maximise the possibilities of God's work within the confines of where people are. A group filled with people who have sought God for themselves and come filled with His Spirit and keen to bless others will be a different group from one where the individuals are battling with habitual sins. That's just the nature of the spiritual life. Group members do not come with gauges demonstrating the degree of Spirit infilling on any given week, nor do they have words displayed on their foreheads suggesting what disposition is most prominent.

Your role is to facilitate the group, however it is configured, so that godliness becomes attractive and sin loathsome, with the hope that all will move forward in their walk with God. You will be praying that He might refresh and excite you and enable the group to function, and that He will be seen as the group meets in His name and for His purposes.

You will, therefore, be making subliminal assessments of the people in your group. Over time you will get to sense where they are in their walk with Christ. These are the kinds of things we pick up, not to make unhealthy judgments but so we can be wise in how to help them, and pray for God to work in them.

We must beware presumption and our own blind spots when it comes to assessing anyone. But we have a role as overseers. In Hebrews it says: 'Have confidence in your leaders and submit to their authority, because they keep watch over you as those who must give an account. Do this so that their work will be a joy, not a burden, for that would be of no benefit to you' (Heb. 13:17).

Paul also speaks of the overseeing role of leaders: 'Keep watch over yourselves and all the flock of which the Holy Spirit has made you overseers' (Acts 20:28).

If we are concerned with what we see in someone, we need to pray and ask for wisdom on whether anything needs to be said. Of course, this also depends on our relationship with them.

In a book like this, you might expect an opportunity to reflect on group members and the degree to which they are walking with Christ. I am not sure it is wise to make assessments in that kind of way, and certainly not to write them down. Even if you were able to make a God-honouring, accurate assessment, this will change over time. But I do think it is appropriate for you to look at the things that God is doing in individual lives as points for praise and prayer, and for you to assess the degree of openness in the group, where real issues can be addressed and blockages to the work of God identified. Here are some questions that might aid you in this:

- Do you know how members regard their own walk with Christ?
- How might you have a conversation with them, without it seeming as if you are prying?

- Does your group have close friends with whom they share their walk with God?
- If your group is attended by non-believers, do they have friends they can talk with about God?
- As you think of your group as individuals, what do you thank God for?
- As you spend time in prayer, are there things that God brings to mind to pray for?

Inviting God's involvement through prayer

There are many examples in the Bible of people gathering where God, in response to their prayers, is present and moving.

In Acts 4:23–31, the believers' prayer led to the house where they were meeting to 'shake'. In Acts 12, Peter's friends prayed fervently for him and he was miraculously released from prison. When people gather to pray in faith for a situation, God is faithful to His promise. So let us explore how prayer in our small groups can help each person to grow and see God move.

As a basis of prayer, it is valuable to reflect on the idea of 'authority' as shown in the Bible. This is a very quick run through of a few scriptures...

We initially had authority. We were to spread God's love and goodness (see Gen. 1:26). But when we sinned, we gave Satan authority, by relinquishing our authority and agreeing with him instead of God. In Scripture, we see God's redemptive work, which begins with Abraham and continues through Israel, as He proves that His Word can be relied upon, and throughout the Old Testament we see God demonstrate His authority.

In the Gospels, we see that Christ comes and that He has authority over all things (eg Luke 10:17–20). After the resurrection, Jesus addresses His followers and tells them that He has all authority (Matt. 28:16–20). Moreover, Paul tells us that Christ 'is the head over every power and authority' (Col. 2:10).

In the light of this, we need to know that we pray in the name of the one who has all authority. And so we can expect something to change as a result. Our challenge is that we do not live at a time when that authority is fully seen and known as it will be in heaven. It is not a simple case of praying and God doing exactly what we ask, nor is it a case of praying and God ignoring us. Someone put it like this: Jesus has all authority but this authority is not always exercised. He will not always intervene now but one day, when He returns, He will act in full authority and judgment.

Imagine that there are some building developments due to take place in your neighbourhood. The owner of the company visits you and you have the opportunity to talk with the one with overall authority about what you like and do not like. Surely you would think about what you wanted to say, and take the whole process seriously. We bring the same kind of seriousness to prayer, except that the one in charge is building His kingdom and invites us to work with Him. This kind of attitude can transform our approach to prayer times and increase our sense of faith that God cares for us and answers prayer.

Why pray?

Scripture encourages us to 'Devote yourselves to prayer, being watchful and thankful' (Col. 4:2) and to 'pray in the Spirit on all occasions with all kinds of prayers and requests' (Eph. 6:18).

Here are some reasons why we may pray in our small groups:

- To receive what we need (Matt. 7:11; John 15:7–8)
- To resist temptation (Matt. 26:41)
- To listen to God, and for wisdom (James 1:5)
- To request forgiveness (1 John 2:1)
- To thank, praise and worship God (1 Thess. 5:18)
- For strength to speak (Col. 4:2–4)
- For courage to witness (Acts 4:31)
- For guidance (Col. 1:9)
- For power to live (Eph. 3:14–19)
- For personal growth to maturity (Col. 4:12)

Also, as a leader, do not underestimate the importance of your own personal prayer life when it comes to leading your group. In Jim Egli's extensive research, which involved over 3,000 small group leaders from more than 200 churches in the United States, he found that of those who said they had a dynamic prayer life, over 80% had seen at least one person come to faith through their small group, whereas less than 20% who said they had a weak prayer life could say the same.

Leading prayer times

Here are a few things to consider about praying in your small group...

First, what are you going to pray about? Sometimes praying is just talking and listening to God with no motive other than to speak and hear from your Father in heaven, just like speaking to an earthly father needs no motivation other than wanting a chat. But you might want to encourage your group to pray particular types of prayer for a short time. There are 'praising prayers', 'petitionary prayers' and 'confessional prayers', among others. Why not have a few minutes of thanking God for things you have learned in the session? Or why not end with confessional prayer in smaller groups, if appropriate?

We have noted how vital it is that leaders pray for their members. It is also vital that members pray for each other and that the goodness, grace and kindness of God become the compelling aspects of your life together. If someone is ill, pray for healing. Look for answers for each other. Ask God what we need to learn. Small groups can be a great place to learn how to give and receive words. Believers can learn the art of hearing God for others in a context of love and grace, where mistakes can be made with minimum fuss.

Second, how are you going to pray? Will you pray as a whole group or will you split into twos and threes? If your group has more than ten people, you might decide to split the group for prayers. It will also depend a little on what space is available where you are meeting.

As the leader, it is always wise to avoid 'prayer language'. There is a lot of prayer jargon that obscures what we do and it can be confusing to newcomers. Phrases that might work well are, 'Let's ask God...' or 'Let's talk to God about...' I believe we often switch off when we use religious language. We forget what is meant by certain terms, and how precious they are.

What also needs considering is whether everyone in the group is comfortable with praying out loud. It is not unusual if a group has at least one person who does not find praying out loud easy. Here are some tips you could try:

- Talk about it. You can ease the pressure on those who are reluctant by assuring them that there is no 'set way'. Prayer is not a chance to parade eloquence or insights into theology.

- Ask those who are silent how they find prayer times in the group, and do so one-to-one. It may be that they would pray out loud but struggle to get a word in edgeways. It may be that they are in a tough season and find it hard to pray at the moment.
- Invite those who are silent to prepare a prayer that they can pray out loud.
- Use set prayers from time to time, so that everyone is praying written prayers.
- If you have people in the group who dominate the time of prayer, or if you have limited time, pray one-sentence prayers.

Here are some key verses surrounding the topic of prayer for you to use or share with your group...

When to pray

'Do not be anxious about anything, but in every situation, by prayer and petition, with thanksgiving, present your requests to God. And the peace of God, which transcends all understanding, will guard your hearts and your minds in Christ Jesus.' (Phil. 4:6–7)

How to pray

'This, then, is how you should pray:
"Our Father in heaven,
hallowed be your name,
your kingdom come,
your will be done,
on earth as it is in heaven.
Give us today our daily bread.
And forgive us our debts,
as we also have forgiven our debtors.
And lead us not into temptation,

but deliver us from the evil one."

For if you forgive other people when they sin against you, your heavenly Father will also forgive you. But if you do not forgive others their sins, your Father will not forgive your sins.'

(Matt. 6:9–15)

The authority of prayer

'Believe me when I say that I am in the Father and the Father is in me; or at least believe on the evidence of the works themselves. Very truly I tell you, whoever believes in me will do the works I have been doing, and they will do even greater things than these, because I am going to the Father. And I will do whatever you ask in my name, so that the Father may be glorified in the Son. You may ask me for anything in my name, and I will do it.' (John 14:11–14)

Praying and having faith

'If any of you lacks wisdom, you should ask God, who gives generously to all without finding fault, and it will be given to you. But when you ask, you must believe and not doubt, because the one who doubts is like a wave of the sea, blown and tossed by the wind. That person should not expect to receive anything from the Lord. Such a person is double-minded and unstable in all they do.'

(James 1:5–8)

06: Let God speak through His Word

I once had the opportunity to interview Rob Bell, the former pastor of Mars Hill Bible Church, Michigan. I chose to speak with him about preaching, since Rob was widely regarded as one of the finest communicators in the US. I began by asking him how he approaches a passage of the Bible. His eyes sparkled as he answered: 'I start with the assumption that this text is electric; that it has things for me to find that will excite and thrill me!'

There are wonderful truths to be found in the Bible regarding the love of God for humanity, seen and appreciated in Christ – truths that have cosmic significance. At the heart of what we are doing in the classic Bible study is hearing this God address us as we read His Word and look to understand and obey what He says.

There are many books and guides available that can assist you in reading, discussing and understanding a Bible passage. In this chapter, we will look at how we can actually create a study from scratch.

What are the aims of a Bible study?

A foundational verse for us can be 2 Timothy 3:14–17:

> 'But as for you, continue in what you have learned and have become convinced of, because you know those from whom you learned it, and how from infancy you have known the Holy Scriptures, which are able to make you wise for salvation through faith in Christ Jesus. All Scripture is God-breathed and is useful for teaching, rebuking, correcting and training in righteousness, so that the servant of God may be thoroughly equipped for every good work.'

Here Paul is giving us a summary verse to describe Scripture. It tells us that the Scriptures are God breathed, meaning that God was at work even as the human authors wrote and in some cases collated and edited existing material. They wrote using the literary conventions of their day, in various styles including narrative, poetry, law, prophecy and apocalyptic. Some authors employ more than one style within a single book. Collectively these scriptures, rightly understood, make us 'wise for salvation through faith in Christ Jesus'. They reach their culmination in the life of Jesus and, as they speak of Him, they are a means by which we put our confidence in Jesus to save us from sin and enable us to live a righteous life.

If this is what the Bible does for us, then living a righteous life should be our key aim in reading and discussing it. The aim is not just Bible knowledge, but the knowledge of God. That is to not only know *about* Him, but to *know Him* as a person, and to see Him as the leader of our life.

What do we mean by 'study'?

Some people may have a negative reaction to the word 'study', perhaps because of bad memories of school. The good news is that the Bible does not actually encourage us to study it in an academic fashion. Academic study has taught us to hold what we are studying at arm's length. In English, we scrutinise the great novelists and poets. In history, we look at what great writers of the past had to say about the times in which they lived. But the Bible is a different kind of book. The God who made us wants us to realise that it is *our* book, which we use to know and enjoy His love for us. The image is more a son enjoying his dad's wise and life-giving words, than an academic critiquing its content.

You may recall that Jesus criticised the Pharisees, 'You study the Scriptures diligently because you think that in them you have eternal life. These are the very Scriptures that testify about me' (John 5:39). They were good 'students' at one level, but completely missed the point.

A better word than 'study' might be 'meditate'. On 60 occasions, the Bible tells us to 'meditate' on the Word of God, which means to mull over and reflect upon it with the purpose of living it. As James puts it: 'Do not merely listen to the word, and so deceive yourselves. Do what it says' (James 1:22).

Our role as a leader of a Bible study is to help those who gather to hear God through His Word. You are there to help shine a light on what God is saying.

Creating a Bible study

First things first, give yourself enough time to create and prepare a Bible study. Start a week if not longer before your meeting. Pray for God's guidance as you pick a passage of Scripture.

Once you have your passage, read it in a few different versions of the Bible. Bible translators all make a decision about whether they translate word for word, which can make the English flow less smoothly, or thought for thought, which is less 'literal' but aims to give the sense of the original meaning. Word-for-word translations include the King James Version, the Amplified Bible and the English Standard Version. Thought-for-thought versions include *The Message* and the New Living Translation.

Although you do not need to know the original Bible languages (Hebrew and a little Aramaic for the Old Testament, and Greek in the New Testament) to lead a Bible study, you can use Bible study aids, such as a Bible concordance, to further grasp what the text is saying. This can often help you determine what was intended by the author, as well as the significance of certain words used.

Having read the passage in different versions, you are ready to start framing your group questions. There are three kinds of questions that will unlock every passage of Scripture: observation questions (what does it say?), interpretation questions (what does it mean?) and application questions (what does it mean for my life?). These are the ones to ask yourself before you suggest questions for the group.

So take one of the most famous passages in the whole Bible: 'For God so loved the world that he gave his one and only Son, that whoever believes in him shall not perish but have eternal life' (John 3:16). Here's how we could study it...

Observation – What does it say?

The answer may be obvious, but answering it helps us to get focused. For this verse we could observe that it says that God loves the world so much that He sent His Son so that human beings like you and me could put our confidence in Him. Because of Jesus, rather than our lives being good for nothing, we have new life, now and forever.

Interpretation – What does it mean?

There are lots of things to potentially draw out. Who is the God who 'loves' the world, according to John? What is the relationship between this God and the 'Son'? What does it mean to 'perish'? Does this mean hell; what kind of place is that? What does 'believe' mean? Is this a cognitive acceptance? What are the implications? What if I have doubts? What kind of life is 'eternal life'?

Application – What does it mean for my life?

This particular verse encourages us to decide whether we believe in Jesus – and this is critical to whether we perish or have eternal life. If eternal life starts now, what does that look like? How can we live in the light of it?

These questions can form the basis of any study. You can frame them to help your group grapple with the text and hear from God. You can spend more time on one question than others. The passage itself will govern the kind of questions you think are needed.

In some cases, just asking people 'What does it say?' might be too basic, so sometimes it might be better to ask a question that will build on a basic question. For example, instead of asking, 'Where were the disciples?' when the answer is clearly 'Capernaum', you could ask, 'How might the disciples have been feeling in Capernaum?'

In non-narrative passages, such as the Psalms or prophecy, you will need questions expanding on 'What does it say?' For example, you might feel the language is worth exploring.

The interpretation questions are always critical and we may have to do some work on the passage within its literary genre and the intention of the author. Remember the Bible is not written *to* us, but *for* us. The application questions will sometimes follow closely from the interpretation, though the breadth of application may mean the Holy Spirit applies it in different ways to people depending on their life circumstance. In some cases, application can be a tricky process.

One helpful method is to ask whether the implications of the text are necessary, probable, improbable or impossible. Necessary implications are those that are almost definitely meant by the author, probable implications are those that the author was likely to have meant, improbable are implications the author is not likely to have meant, and impossible are implications that the author almost certainly did not mean at all. For example, take 'Do not commit adultery'. It definitely means 'do not have sexual relations with a person who is not your spouse'. It probably means 'be careful of situations in which you and someone who is not your spouse are alone together'. It is improbable that it means 'do not ever have lunch with someone who is not your spouse'; and it is impossible that it means 'do not have dinner with another couple because you are at the same table with someone who is not your spouse'.

Part of your job as leader is to use questions that will help the group hear God for themselves. There may be occasions where you need to share the breadth of interpretation of a passage when there is a disagreement within the wider body of Christ. On occasions, you may want to share any line that the local church takes. This is especially important if someone seems overly dogmatic about a doctrine or approach. Your job is not to accomplish unanimity, but to aid wise interpretation. Comments like 'You may want to reconsider' or 'You might like to know that many Christians take another view there' might be the kind of peace-making language you need.

Variation on question and answer Bible studies

There may be occasions when you fancy a change from the classic Bible study approach, and there may be occasions when events in the week overtake you and you discover that the time you had for preparation was eaten up. The good news is that these approaches require minimal time for preparation.

Manuscript Bible study

Using www.manuscriptbiblestudy.com or another Bible text website, find a few chapters, such as one of Paul's shorter letters, the Sermon on the Mount (Matt. 5–7) or the upper room discourse (John 14–17). Making sure there are no headings, chapter and verse divisions (and ideally, double space the text), print out a copy of the text for each member of the group.

During the meeting, hand everyone the Bible text and give them the following instructions:

- Read through the text a few times on your own and, as you do, ask: Who is there? What is happening? When is it? Where is it? How is it happening?
- Use coloured pens to highlight or circle key words or ideas.
- Think about the flow of thought and then write a brief title for each paragraph.
- Look at the context of the passage. What comes before and after it in the Bible?
- Think about those questions again and look hard in the passage for insights.
- Then come together as a group and share your findings.

You will need to give people plenty of time to read, highlight and think. The speed of discovery will depend on the Bible knowledge of the group, but you should perhaps give at least 30 minutes.

The Swedish Method

This method is so named because the creator first used this approach with Swedish students.

Begin your study by praying, asking God to speak through His Word. Then read a short Bible passage aloud (10–15 verses is ideal). Instruct each person to go back over the passage on their own while being on the lookout for three things:

- A 'light bulb': This should be something that 'shines' from the passage – whatever impacts most, or draws attention.
- A 'question mark': Anything that is difficult to understand in the text, or a question the reader would like to ask the writer of the passage, or God.
- An 'arrow': A personal application for the reader's life.

The group members should write down at least one thing for each. Allow people time to savour the text and explore it at their own speed. This usually takes about ten minutes, in silence. You can then discuss what you have all found. First by looking at the 'light bulbs', then the 'question marks', and lastly by discussing the 'arrows', applying it to your own lives. The philosophy behind this style of Bible reading is to promote good observation of the text, group participation and self-guided discovery.

DIY topical Bible study

Explore a particular theme or topic by using books and resources such as a Bible concordance, dictionary, lexicon or commentary (many are available online).

Begin the group with a statement about the theme and then allow the group to come up with questions they may have about it. Then investigate using the resources you have, coming back together to share your findings.

You may decide to set a topic one week for the following week so that reading can be carried out at home.

Dramatic reading

Select a narrative text with a number of characters involved. Allocate 'parts' out to the group and read through the text together. A dramatised Bible would be ideal, but any Bible could be used.

After a couple of readings, the characters and narrator (if there is one) reflect on their own roles in the drama and fill in more about how the character might have been thinking and feeling.

If the group is too large for all to participate, consider splitting the group to double up on the characters.

DVD-based studies

This is a question and answer approach with a difference. A short presentation via DVD is interspersed with questions, or has questions to ask the group at the end to help facilitate discussion. CWR produces lots of DVDs useful for this kind of study, including *7 Laws for Life*, *Life Journeys with Jeff Lucas* and *Faith, Hope, Love and Everything in Between*.

Your task as leader is to help the discussion, and it is almost always helpful for you to have seen the DVD episode before the group meet so that you can think about tailoring the discussion to suit your group.

Audio Bible

Take a portion of the Bible and either play an audio recording or ask someone in the group to read it aloud. It may be several chapters from the Bible, such as Matthew 5–7, John 14–15, Genesis 1–2 or Nehemiah 1–2.

At the end of the reading, ask the group what the passage was about and what they remember.

Read the passage again and see if the group can fill in the parts that they missed.

Ask the group what they have learned for themselves from the exercise.

On the spot

Here we seek to test the group's ability to explain and explore an idea to someone who is not yet a believer. You can make the questions as simple or as difficult as you like, depending on the group. You ideally need to have prepared yourself beforehand, so you can give an idea of how you would have answered. The group should be encouraged to demonstrate their answers from the Bible where they can. Here are some questions you could start with:

- How can I begin to trust Jesus?
- Why does my sin need to be forgiven?
- What did the crucifixion of Jesus accomplish?
- Why should I think the Bible is reliable?

07: Lead your meetings well

The doorbell sounds, heralding that the first person has arrived. You have planned and prepared, but the live event that you are about to host is always wonderfully unpredictable. In this chapter, we will look at some key aspects of the group meetings themselves, and consider how we can facilitate effective meetings. If you are running an activity-based group or course group, there are some further tips at the end of this chapter.

Leading a classic small group

Setting the tone
You set the tone for your time together. You have prayed about the evening and have prepared the material, so ideally you look forward to playing the role of facilitating the chance for people to meet with God and connect with each other. Your role is to be expectant for what will happen. (If someone else is actually leading the study part, you still have a leadership role, overseeing what goes on.)

That all sounds good in theory. In practice you might be unprepared, have forgotten to pray and are looking forward to it being over! I stress the *ideal* attitude because an approach that is faith-filled and optimistic can help you overcome any nerves and uncertainties. I find that if I am focused on the text and what I am looking for God to do, I quickly forget any diffidence I have and lose myself in what is about to happen. Of course, the success of the time does not depend totally on your attitude, but if you are bored and apathetic, and would rather be elsewhere, the group has a mountain to climb if they are to benefit!

Catching up

Most groups have a time of catching up and settling down before a Bible study begins. Try to use this time to talk to as many of the group as you can. You may be tempted to talk with those you like, those you know and those who are easy to talk to, but resist this in favour of looking to connect with anyone who is not easily mixing with others, so that everyone feels welcome and comfortable within the group. If you discover that someone has news that really needs more wider sharing (good or bad), then encourage them to share it. Remember, everyone has their right to privacy and not everyone will want to disclose their life at the same level. (Later we will look at the value of connecting outside of meetings so that you can build meaningful relationships.)

Welcoming newcomers

On occasions it may be necessary to integrate a newcomer into the group. New people in the group is good news – you have another person who is keen to enjoy small group life and the group can be refreshed with a new member. Of course, it is a challenge too.

Some groups get very comfortable with the people they share the group with, and there may be some adjusting before everyone feels comfortable with each other.

To help aid this time you could invite the newcomer to say something about their life within the first few occasions, but only if they are happy to. This will probably include how they came to faith and how they came to be in the church. Knowing a little about their past can facilitate connection with the rest of the group. If they clearly find any public speaking very difficult, you could have a chat with them and then summarise the story for the group.

Introduce the newcomer to general things about the group such as what happens, the aims of the group, how they might contribute and so on.

Make a note to ask them how they are settling in after two or three meetings. They may seem to be happy, but it is still worth asking. Give them a chance to ask you questions too. Also, note and monitor the impact the newcomer has on the group. It may not be easily discerned at first, but if some are reacting to their presence negatively, you will need to address it sensitively and wisely.

Sharing testimonies

Telling brief life stories is good practice for everyone. If you are starting a completely new group, it is a great way of breaking the ice. Whether sharing recent testimonies (such as stories of evangelism or healing) or past testimonies (such as stories of how you came to faith, etc), ensure your group knows that every person has the right to decide what they share and what they do not share with the group.

It often helps if you share first. Telling something of your story may help the group connect with you, and it also leads the way for them to feel comfortable with sharing as well. A relaxed approach to this time will help facilitate openness.

Storytelling may also overcome some cultural barriers among the members. It sometimes overcomes prejudice and dispels ignorance. Knowing the trials and highpoints of another person's life is powerful in bonding a group.

Often this time provides a great opportunity for prayer ministry within the life of the group too.

Serving the group

It is important to recognise that you serve both the whole group and the individual attendees. It is a bit of a dancing act. You may need to ask yourself at any moment of the meeting: 'Is this benefiting everyone? Is this involving everyone?'

So keep things moving, but be careful not to rush things if it is clear there is valuable discussion going on. Watch out for body language and verbal cues that may suggest a member is not engaged with discussion or activity. Try not to single them out in front of the group but subtly ask them how they feeling or what they are thinking.

Responding to the moment

Your role is to facilitate discussion and learning. All sorts of questions will arise, thoughts will be expressed, and opinions shared. On many occasions you will be able to deal with things that arise at the time.

If someone expresses a view not backed by Scripture, you could say, 'Does anyone have a view on that?' in the hope that someone in the group is prepared to pitch in. If they do not, you may need to express a view along the lines, 'Are you sure? I wonder if you have considered...'

You want people to say what they think. But if there is disagreement and it is clear that it is not going to be resolved, you could always suggest that the conversation is continued on another occasion. Your job as the leader is to be positive about the prospect of a good outcome.

If a topic comes up that you had not expected, you could say 'Can we revisit that another time?' or 'That may be too deep for us to get into here' or, if you are happy to proceed, spend a few minutes on it but be wary not to get too side-tracked.

Remember you can always deal with things at a later or more appropriate time, inside or outside of the group setting, inviting dialogue and aiming for fellowship and growth in Christ.

Another thing to note is, you will have planned the questions you want the group to consider, but as the evening progresses you may well have supplementary questions to add. You want to ask open-ended questions such as, 'What do you think about following Jesus?' as opposed to closed questions like, 'Do you think Jesus wants us to follow Him?'

Keeping an eye on the time
As you plan the evening, you may need to have some kind of idea of how long the study will take. You will want to avoid the two extremes: being the time warrior who has everything timed to the minute and rushes to the next question regardless, and being the happy go lucky type, who allows the evening to meander aimlessly according to the whims of the group.

When it comes to your Bible study, it may help to have in your head the 'worst case scenario'. For example, we only have time for three out eight questions. So which ones would you choose? If you happen to get through questions more speedily than you had intended, you can spend longer time on the application and if necessary get everyone in the group to say something, leading into a time of prayer.

Time spent will also be influenced by how chatty the group are, and by how much energy they have. Your role as leader is to sense what God is doing in and with the group, when to linger on an area that seems to be resonating and when to move on.

Closing well

Some group members may be less bothered than others about time-keeping and when a meeting should end. But as leader, be respectful of everyone's time – especially those who may have arranged childcare so that they can be there.

Closing well may mean summarising how you feel the evening has gone. On the rare occasion when there has been tension, disagreement or awkwardness of any kind, you may want to make reference to that, and pray accordingly. You may want to give opportunity for further prayer. Others may want to thank God for an aspect of the study that helped them that you would not necessarily have thought of. This is also a great time to mention arrangements for the next meeting and any wider church meetings that people need to know about.

Leading a course small group

Courses may be as short as a few weeks, or as long as a whole term. They are a different kind of small group: attendees are a 'group' for just a short time. I am thinking here of courses such as debt recovery, parenting, Christian discovery (Alpha, Christianity Explored, The Y-Course, Emmaus), marriage enrichment and so on.

The first five minutes of a meeting are pretty critical. Everyone may be a little unsure of what to expect and any non-believers may be especially nervous, so this is the time to introduce the leaders, explain what the course is aiming to do and what the expectations of the attendees may be. Where possible, announce what each evening will cover and what the format is.

You may know how many are intending to attend, and have appropriate books, booklets or handouts. If it is possible for people to join the course after the first week, say so, as people may want to bring others along next time.

If you are using PowerPoint or other audio-visual media, you will need to ensure that this works in good time. If you are using an unfamiliar building, try to check that all is working before the day (if you can). If you have your own materials as a backup, take them!

When you come to the end of the course, it is a good idea to ask attendees how the time has been for them. It gives you a chance to tweak or change things for next time.

Leading an activity small group

Groups based around activities can be the most attractive to those outside the faith. The shared activity brings people together and there is no obligation for them to do or say anything remotely 'religious'.

It is important to recognise that the group still needs to be led in some way. Someone still needs to plan, pray, monitor, assess, reflect, adjust, and do the things a leader does. The activity may be relaxed, and less obviously 'spiritual', but God regards the time as a place where He can work if we invite and welcome Him. Make sure that the strategy is clear. Activity-based small groups are a great opportunity for Christians and non-believers to get together and develop connections. Leaders need to be praying that connection takes place, and inform the group members of the other options within the church, if only by handing out a leaflet, notice or schedule. Non-believers might then find opportunities to explore the faith in addition to conversation with believers.

That said, it is good to be clear that the group is connected to the church. The aim of the group is not to be so incognito that the attendee discovers after the fifth week that all the attendees are Christians and have been fasting and praying that they come to faith!

You do not have to avoid 'God talk' either. Non-believers are often more interested in what we believe than we imagine, and it would be foolish for Christians to live as if Jesus is a secret to be kept. Every group has its own atmosphere of course and you will be able to sense what is appropriate. But try not to be so nervous about putting off a non-believer that you do not mention God at all. I have found it helpful to distinguish between conversations that expose faith and impose faith.

When we expose faith, we are simply talking about our walk with God – our recent personal testimony. We are not telling listeners that they need to embrace this faith for themselves, simply exposing our faith. We impose faith when we share our faith in a way that invites the person to embrace the faith we have. Of course, there is a place for this kind of conversation too.

It may be helpful to remember Peter's words in this:

'But in your hearts revere Christ as Lord. Always be prepared to give an answer to everyone who asks you to give the reason for the hope that you have. But do this with gentleness and respect, keeping a clear conscience, so that those who speak maliciously against your good behaviour in Christ may be ashamed of their slander.' (1 Pet. 3:15–16)

08: Allow people to flourish

We are all capable of harbouring unhelpful character traits. These can manifest themselves in small group situations, stunting an individual's spiritual growth, and perhaps the group's as a knock-on effect. In this chapter, we will look at some of these traits or characteristics, and consider how we can respond in such a way that will help individuals and the group as a whole.

We are called to 'accept one another' and 'bear with one another', so nothing that follows is intended to mean that we should label or define someone by a behaviour trait, or avoid people we find challenging. I have titled this chapter as I have because, in many cases, the individual and group cannot flourish if we leave certain traits unchecked. Interactions between people are not merely between two humans – God uses us to help form others and others to help form us; He wants to be involved in every interaction.

At the very start of our discussion, we need to flag up the need to have an upfront and honest conversation with anyone about behaviour that is causing concern. Below I will outline some approaches, but there is no substitute for a simple one-to-one chat. Such conversations can seem daunting. A good way to start one is with the assumption that you may be wrong about what you are observing. You state the situation based on facts: 'I have noticed that this happens. This is what this does to the group' (or an individual in the group). You then ask, 'Are you aware of this? Do you think this is a fair observation?' If they agree you can ask whether they could make some changes in their behaviour for the sake of the group. You can offer to support them, if necessary. If they question your version or are unaware of it and become defensive, the fact that you have brought it up may moderate their behaviour.

Of course, try not be accusing or intense in the conversation. This advice may sound trite, and you will know that some people find any questioning of how they relate extremely difficult to discuss, so take care as you broach the subject, and do it prayerfully.

Responding to certain traits

Manipulating

The problem: The person seems to have another agenda from that which you set as the group leader, but this is not obvious and so is hard to pin down.

Response: By its very nature, manipulating behaviour is hard to respond to because the manipulator is deliberately keeping their behaviour secret. If you suspect someone is looking to be manipulative, you can ask them outright, 'Are you looking to...' They may deny it, in which case you can explain why you assumed they were. And if they really are being manipulative, they are unlikely to continue.

Controlling

The problem: The person has a strong view on how things should be and looks to change the group.

Response: Try and get them on your side if you can. Explain that you (or the church) have decided on the present approach. If the way they want to lead seems good, then look for opportunities to involve them in leading sessions, or suggest that they look to lead a group themselves. Do not be intimidated.

Confronting

The problem: In some cases, if someone confronts another for the purpose of spiritual growth, this is a good thing. Paul confronted Peter when he perceived hypocrisy in Peter's dealings with the 'Circumcision Party'. The problem is when a person confronts others unhelpfully and you sense some sort of ulterior agenda.

Response: They will need to be reminded of Jesus' teaching and be asked to make sure they have the correct attitude, and their facts right, before they bring accusations against others. If this is in a church culture where their behaviour is especially unusual, you can point that out to them.

Argumentative

The problem: We want groups that are prepared to have disagreements should people differ in their views. But problems occur when a person takes the opposite view again and again for no apparent reason.

Response: A simple comment such as: 'You're playing devil's advocate again, aren't you?' might work. It depends on the topic you are studying, but there will be times when there should be no argument and it might be good as a leader to celebrate those moments. If there is an occasion when the argumentative behaviour has left someone shaken or upset, you can reflect with them on what happened and how you are looking as a group to build peace.

Problem dumping

The problem: The person sharing seems fixated on their issues and takes up significant time airing them, with no useful outcome for them or for the rest of the group.

Response: The small group is a place to be open and share. But if someone shares information about problems repeatedly, or returns to the same issues over and over again, they really need to address these outside of the group. This may be with you, someone close to them, someone in the pastoral care team, or a counsellor. You could ask them to talk about it with you later and help them arrange a time.

Divisive

The problem: The kind of divisiveness you may encounter might be in the form of criticism of the church's main leader, the church leadership as a whole, a group within the church, or an approach the church has taken towards an issue. This is probably not a bid on the part of the critic, to split the church asunder, but it still needs to be taken seriously.

Response: Saying nothing implies acquiescence with the view. On occasions you may be able to speak in defence of the person being criticised, but they may be looking for validation that their view is correct. It is not your place to take sides, but it is your place to urge reconciliation.

People pleasing

The problem: The people pleaser does not seem to ever connect with the group. They emit a charming persona, but you wonder whether they ever have any views of their own. They are often aiming to please others out of a low self-image and belief that if they simply comply, they will not be criticised.

Response: Encourage the people pleaser to say what they really think. But really helping them is likely to take more in-depth knowledge of who they are, which can only be gleaned from time outside the group, where they build trust with you and can feel able to let down their guard.

Passive

The problem: This person never or rarely volunteers a contribution or action. They may seem absentminded and lacking true emotion.

Response: Some people are nervous in social situations and are comfortable not saying much. That has got to be OK. But you do need to check if they are quiet because they want to be, and not for another reason such as being in a season of life that means they are reluctant to share. Might they want to speak one on one? It may be that there are too many talkers in the group. Would they like to be invited to answer sometimes? Are they reluctant to appear foolish? You can stress that there are no 'silly questions' or 'silly comments' – we all learn together.

Are there other traits that you have identified in the past or present? How might you define the problem and frame a response?

_____

_____

_____

_____

_____

Responding to certain moods

It is sometimes tricky to talk of traits with respect to people. It can be even more problematic to talk in terms of the overall mood of a group. After all, any group is made up of individuals with their constantly switching moods and outlooks, which adjust and so create various moods each time they meet.

Some moods, or group dynamics, can become unhelpful. So how do we respond to these? Here are a few examples of problematic moods and how we might respond to them in a way that can bring about positive change.

Superficial

The problem: People attend the group but show little commitment to one another. Relationships seem stuck at surface level and people are not engaging with deeper, more meaningful discussions. It appears that certain needs in the group are not being sufficiently expressed.

Response: It is important to know that this is a stage many groups go through. It can take a while for people to integrate. Sometimes people are not committed to each other because they are not yet really committed to the Lord. Sometimes people need to know what commitment to one another looks like. Over time, you can lead by example and pray that love for the Lord increases and flows to and through people. John reminds us that we cannot claim to love God if we do not love his people (1 John 4:20).

Disconnected and individualistic

The problem: This mood fits with the earlier one, but is really about people choosing not to connect with others. It is very much the spirit of the age, but often flows from people who have not learned the value of giving and receiving from others.

Response: We are made to 'know and be known'; this is intrinsic to who we are as people. So whatever you can do to encourage connection will be for everyone's good. Can you invite some over for a meal? Can you share personal stories one evening? Are there some 'bonding' activities you could do together?

Fragmented

The problem: Various cliques have formed in the group, causing disunity and even leaving some feeling unwelcome or secluded. Those in a clique may not even be aware of it.

Response: We should encourage people to be close to one another, and recognise that smaller groups may form when people share personal information not appropriate within the wider group. But if this kind of connection is negatively affecting the group, you may want to have a conversation with some members about including others in the group.

Conflicted

The problem: Two or more people in the group regularly argue. Even when just two people do not get on, it can affect everyone. Some may side with one, some with the other, many may just be upset with the tense atmosphere.

Response: Somehow you have to ask the two people to sort it out (according to the advice in Matt. 18). Offer to be involved yourself, or find a mediator. If they are unable to resolve the issue, they may have to leave the group. I would sometimes suggest that both leave, unless they agree otherwise, because if one stays they may feel vindicated, and the other punished.

Stuck

The problem: The group feels stuck in a rut – whether with the Bible study or even more generally. Perhaps you have not had any new members for a long while and things are feeling a little stagnant or just comfortable. (This may be the very reason why you are reading this book!)

Response: Hopefully, what you have read so far in this book will help, particularly the first two chapters where you consider your purpose and vision. Have you considered a radical change? A completely new topic for a term, a change in evening format, a meeting to discuss what works and what does not, a week of prayer and fasting? Whatever you choose, tell yourself that no action is not an option.

Insular

The problem: We have noted before how groups can sometimes create an atmosphere and sense of belonging that makes the group resistant to welcoming newcomers, which puts off newcomers altogether. If there is no expectation of group growth, this can be hard to change in the short term.

Response: Over time, introduce the idea that the group needs to be more open to newcomers and that this is the approach taken throughout the church. You might even discuss what challenges and opportunities that will bring. Pray as a group for new people to come and that they will feel welcome.

Disintegrating

The problem: Sometimes it is just not possible to improve a small group. Perhaps repeated attempts to revitalise the group with new members or with ways of doing things have not worked. Perhaps members consistently behave in ways not keeping with the faith, and refuse to accept attempts at discipline. Perhaps numbers are dwindling and there are only a very few 'regulars'. The group may be in its final stages before ceasing.

Response: It is not a 'failure' to end a small group. If it is no longer serving God's purposes then it is much better to stop. You might want to have a final meeting, celebrating the good times and praying that each of the members may flourish elsewhere.

Are there other group moods that you have identified in the past or present? How might you define the problem and frame a response?

_____

_____

_____

_____

_____

Pay attention to details

You may have heard of the phrase 'the devil is in the detail', used to describe the way that the smallest thing going wrong can affect everything.

In this chapter, we are going to look at the details of a small group and consider how we can ensure, as much as possible, that problems do not arise because of them. After every detail you will find a few lines. You can use these to jot down your thoughts on each. You may like to consider whether each one is something you already do well, something where there is room for improvement, or something you could perhaps start.

Ground rules

Just as a family may have household rules, small groups also develop conventions, sometimes without seemingly choosing to do so. It is worth thinking about your conventions (or rules) and stating them so they become mutually agreed. Your agreement may include:

- We listen to one another
- What is said in the room stays in the room

- We send apologies for absence
- We pray for one another

These kinds of ground rules will assist everyone. You should not need to be heavy-handed about them. They simply help to ensure wise behaviour. You may choose to say them as a helpful reminder from time to time.

_____

_____

_____

_____

_____

_____

Neighbours

Small groups have to meet somewhere, and many meet in homes. In these instances, it is helpful to consider the neighbours. Are noise levels acceptable for example, or could there be an issue with parking? Many homes are in streets where parking is at a premium and you may find that your road cannot accommodate the cars required. What are your options? You could use another home that has plenty of parking. You could vary the meeting venue, so the frequency of the problem is reduced. You could encourage members to travel together, or park a little further away. You could even knock on the door of your neighbours (or write a letter) and apologise in advance if parking is tricky. It would be one way to get to know the neighbours too!

_____

_____

_____

_____

_____

_____

Communication

Not everyone likes the same method of getting in touch. Some use email daily, others once a week. Some communicate mainly through text messages, others only use their home telephone. Then there is social media messaging to choose from too. Find a way of balancing convenience and everyone's preferences as best you can when it comes to updating members on group meetings. A group message to all is convenient if you are in a rush, but a personalised text or phone call helps members feel connected and valued.

_____

_____

_____

_____

_____

Food and drink

It is always good to have a range of hot and cold drinks on offer, as well as a few savoury and sweet snacks. We can quickly discover what members of the group tend to prefer. Being hospitable and conscientious in this way helps people relax and feel welcome. It is a simple but affirming gesture when you know how someone likes their tea!

If you meet at someone else's house, and often, consider whether you could bring food and drink to help with costs. Some groups take it in turns to bring something. Also, have you ever considered having meals together? One small group I know have a meal together at the start of the meeting and believe it has transformed their gatherings.

_____

_____

_____

_____

_____

_____

Seating and comfort

Ideally, people in the room should be able to see each other (and a TV screen if necessary) and sit comfortably for the duration of the meeting. If any are hard of hearing or have an injury or back problem, this is especially important. Some people are comfortable sitting on the floor for extended periods, but others are not, so make sure there is enough seating. It may be helpful to consider if the room is at a good temperature and has enough ventilation. Also, if the group will split into smaller sub-groups for the prayer time, consider whether there is enough room for this.

_____

_____

_____

_____

_____

_____

Time keeping

For some groups, when they start and end a meeting can be flexible without any adverse effects. For others, such as those groups with parents or young people, we need to be a little more careful. Do you always start on time? If you only start when everyone has arrived, no matter how late, you may find that people start arriving later and later. You might need to be firm and start at the same time each week to shake people out of this pattern. Some people may have babysitters at home, or some may need to be picked up and given a lift home. You, or the host, may have young children that need a quiet house after a certain time. Try and ensure that you end the meeting at a reasonable time. It might be worth asking members, individually, how they find the time keeping in the group, and come to a general agreement.

_____

_____

_____

_____

_____

_____

Bibles

If the small group involves a Bible study, encourage people to bring Bibles, and have some spares to hand (perhaps borrow from the church if necessary). In some cases, you might want to print text off in advance. Almost every English Bible translation (and many in other languages too, if needed) are available online or via smartphone apps. People have their favourite Bible versions, but it may help to use the version preferred at your church, if known. It can often be beneficial to have a couple of different versions in order to get a balanced view of the meaning behind the words.

_____

_____

_____

_____

_____

Printed word

For some, the words 'Bible study' sound intimidating and sitting around discussing a text can be alienating. It is worth being aware of this. You may need to help someone unfamiliar with a book-centred culture to be integrated. If reading is likely to be a struggle, there are other ways of learning and growing. There are audio Bibles and video re-enactments, if you feel that these would aid group members in their engagement with the Bible. In any case, reading is only one part of following Jesus, and in His lifetime it was of less importance than observation and imitation.

_____

_____

_____

_____

_____

_____

Prayer

We looked at prayer in Chapter 5, but one practical consideration is to try and make a note of prayer needs and any answers. As we believe God hears our prayers and answers, we need to remember what we said and adjust or continue our prayers as necessary.

_____

_____

_____

_____

_____

_____

Mobile phones

Today, mobile phones can seem to be attached to us. As they can very easily distract, and sometimes even disrupt, it might be worth agreeing that phones are turned off or on silent, unless there are exceptional circumstances. You can gauge how strict you need to be on this front.

_____

_____

_____

_____

_____

Children

The small group needs to be clear about whether children are welcome and easily accommodated. If the host has children, obviously they need to be well looked after, so as not to be an unnecessary distraction, depending on age and ease with which they could engage with the group.

_____

_____

_____

_____

_____

Culture

Consider people from a cultural background different from your own. When you know that someone from a different culture is likely to be there, it might be worth looking up on any customs, food requirements and social niceties that would make them feel welcome. Of course, try not to go overboard on this as a particular custom might not be for them personally. But if you have done a little homework, at least they will know you care.

_____

_____

_____

_____

_____

_____

Birthdays

It is useful to know people's birthdays within the group. For some, birthdays are very precious. Maybe you could ask for them all during a meeting, and jot them down in your diary? You could make it a habit to organise a card to be signed by everyone for each person's birthday. Some groups organise a gift but that is entirely up to your group. One thing to be sure of is that you try to be fair by doing the same for each person.

_____

_____

_____

_____

_____

_____

Building connections

Do you or could you meet up with members of your group outside of the regular meetings? Building these kinds of connections can be a great foundation for a group that gels well. You will know how easily this can be done depending on your free time, but sometimes a little sacrifice can pay off greatly.

_____

_____

_____

_____

_____

Socials

From time to time, small groups may have evenings or occasions that are different from the normal meeting. Some call them socials. I know many small group leaders who groan inwardly when it comes to the termly social and beat themselves up about them not being better. The first thing to say is that good socials flow from good community. You cannot magically 'create' community by singing karaoke, or going for a picnic. When socials flow from Christian community they can be a great time of connecting, and for involving spouses or friends who do not attend the group but might enjoy a different setting. Here are some ideas for inspiration:

- Pot luck supper – every brings a 'dish' and everyone shares
- Ramble – you will need a map and good shoes. Tough but not impossible in urban areas!
- Film night – you could even choose a film you intend to critique together
- Group day out – at the park or somewhere else in your local community
- Talent night – everyone brings their best party piece
- Book club – everyone has five minutes to talk about a favourite book
- Cinema, theatre, restaurant or sporting occasion trip (be careful about cost)

_____

_____

_____

_____

_____

_____

Expectations

What are your group members expecting when it comes to newcomers? Are they expecting a group that never changes or one where there are new people attending from time to time? We looked at the topic in Chapter 7 but the details needs to be thought through a little more. Many classic small groups have built a degree of trust that makes it hard for them to imagine a newcomer joining without upsetting the close bond that exists. But if groups can be set up for growth from the very start, with the expectation that people may join, you start off on a very different footing. It does not mean the group does not develop appropriate levels of connection, just that you have to be deliberate about how the newcomer is helped to feel at home.

We may think our small group is friendly, which might actually mean 'my small group is friendly towards me'. Newcomers might have an altogether different story. Be wary of too many in-jokes and references to people the newcomer does not know.

Also, consider what the newcomer expects from the group. Why not meet up with them before they start and discuss what your group is about and what you do together? They can share their expectations and, if appropriate, you can ensure they are met.

Allocation

If people can potentially be added to your group, it is worth considering the mechanism whereby this takes place. Are people simply allocated according to set criteria, such as location, numbers in the group, or age? At what point does a group split or groups merge? In theory, all Christians should get on with all others, but you may know that some will thrive in one group rather than another. If necessary, talk with your fellow small group leaders and church leaders if you have any concerns or ideas.

_____

_____

_____

_____

_____

_____

Spiritual mix

Some groups work well with a mixed level of spiritual maturity, whereas some work better when all are on the same level. No one is denying that a Bible study group cannot incorporate people at both ends, with younger believers benefitting from the experience of the more mature and the older from the enthusiasm of the newly born again. But is this the best situation?

If you are a church leader, you will know how valuable it is to meet with other leaders, where some things about church leadership are a given and you can be ministered to at an appropriate level. Perhaps it is best, if small groups are set up to foster spiritual growth, to have people at a similar stages of their journey.

There is also an issue of how we define levels of maturity. Perhaps we could loosely simplify it into three broad groups:

1. Those new to faith (say the first two years)
2. Those maturing as believers learning to live for Christ

3. Those more mature who are disciple makers themselves

Those who are seriously 'disciple making' will have a different set of challenges to those in the other two categories, and will need appropriate fellowship and support for that part of the work.

Consider your group. Is there any tension or imbalance when it comes to spiritual maturity?

_____

_____

_____

_____

_____

_____

10: Take control of your future

There can often be a gap between intention and action. In this chapter, we will consider how we can take the next step in acting on all that we have explored and discovered in this book.

If you believe God is leading you to act on something, consider the following short parable from Matthew 21:28–32:

> '"What do you think? There was a man who had two sons. He went to the first and said, 'Son, go and work today in the vineyard.'
> 'I will not,' he answered, but later he changed his mind and went.
> Then the father went to the other son and said the same thing.
> He answered, 'I will, sir,' but he did not go.
> Which of the two did what his father wanted?"
> "The first," they answered.'

Let us not be like the second son, who did not follow up his words with his actions.

So then, how do we start to bring about change? In their book *Switch* (Random House, 2011), Chip and Dan Heath explain that, for things to change, somebody somewhere has to start acting differently. They use the image of someone riding an elephant and suggest that everyone has an 'emotional' elephant side and a 'rational' rider side. For change to occur, you have to influence both, but the 'emotions' tend to dictate which way you go. It is no good having rational reasons for change if the emotional side of our lives is not satisfied, and vice versa. But the book also outlines the third key element: the route. The rider needs to know the route to take. Too many have been convinced of change, feel they need to change, but not known 'how' and so have remained where they were. This book has hopefully indicated a route to take. It is for you to assess what you are feeling and thinking about the options before you.

Key to moving forward is seeking God's leadership. Take the advice of James, who reminds us that no one can plan as if God were not involved (James 4:13–15). So, take a few moments to look back through all the things you have noted down, and identify those areas that struck you as needing thought, discussion or action. It may be something about leading meetings, preparing studies, or the planning of the group perhaps.

Some things you might have read and thought, 'Yes, that's a good idea. We can improve that' and you can implement these with a minimum of fuss. Other ideas you may need to further prayerfully consider first. There may even be some ideas that could help shape other small groups in your church. (We will look at ideas for a church small group overhaul later in this chapter.)

If you work alongside other leaders, you may need to consult your ideas with them too. They may be your fellow leader, the small group co-ordinator or the senior church leader. When you do so, take care on how you approach them. You have spent time reading this book and may have developed an enthusiasm that they may need time to feel or understand. You can state your ideas about what might be possible, but try to do so in a way that gives them plenty of opportunity to ask questions, and suggest concerns and ways in which the approach can be shaped.

People often say that they do not like change but, in reality, many of us do enjoy change – a new car, job, clothes etc. These are changes we want for ourselves. What we do not enjoy so much is when we feel forced into a change. We can help people *want* to change rather than making them feel like they *have* to change. Your job is to help the other leader recognise what is not working and suggest new ways of acting, but in a way that they can embrace, and therefore join in with.

Goals for my small group

Once you have decided on changes you would like to make, try setting some goals. Goals are a great way of encouraging action. And a means of creating good goals is using the 'SMARTER' approach. This acronym stands for the following:

S: Specific
We can often set goals that are too broad or ambiguous, such as 'I want us to improve our times of Bible study'. Specific goals are precise and clear. In effect, they are much easier to aim for. For example, 'I want to have discussed new methods of Bible study with my co-leaders, reaching a decision on the right one and starting the approach in four weeks' time.'

M: Measurable
Measurable goals are quantifiable. To set a measurable goal, you need to establish concrete criteria for measuring your progress against. For example, rather than 'I want our group to grow',

you could say, 'I want to have welcomed three newcomers to the group in the next six months.'

A: Attainable

Attainable goals are challenging but not so much that they are impossible. To accomplish these, you generally do so by developing certain attitudes, abilities, skills or financial capacities involved. For example, 'I want to encourage group members to overcome their fear of praying aloud by praying a short prayer in the next meeting – the first step in developing this ability'.

R: Relevant

Relevant goals are appropriate for your specific group. If you are a classic small group, you may have differing goals to a leader of a short course small group. For example, a course on debt recovery may have the relevant goal of 'I want our group members to find at least three practical ways of managing their money well during the course'. You could run these goals by your group members to see if they find them relevant, and why.

T: Time-sensitive

Time-sensitive goals have an end point that can be found on a calendar. Time frames tied to your goals provide a sense of urgency to help motivate you.

E: Evaluate

Be sure to evaluate goals regularly and adjust them as needed to account for changes in family, job responsibilities or the availability of resources, for example.

R: Re-do

Re-do goals after the evaluation process and then go through the SMARTER process again to check that you are still happy.

Using the 'SMARTER' approach, write some key goals for your group.

_____

_____

_____

_____

_____

_____

_____

_____

_____

_____

_____

_____

_____

_____

_____

A small group overhaul

It may be that your church is about to begin small groups, or there is a general mood that small groups are not working anymore, and a big overhaul is in mind. So what could you, or indeed you church, do? Here are some options to consider...

Cell church

In the UK, cell churches have had some success. The cell church was made especially famous by Dr David Yonggi Cho, pastor of the Yoido Full Gospel Church in South Korea, which having been founded in the seventies had no less than a million worshippers by the turn of the century.

He sees 'cell' as providing a structure to care for and disciple people. Cell groups meet weekly in homes and come together with other cells as a local body at celebration services. Each small group has a structure within it that enables the leader to be a facilitator.

Churches have found that they are able to maintain an average of one leader to every 10–16 church members. Hence a cell group church has no limit as long as the 'church' is effectively mobilising leaders to minister through cell groups. There are the section leaders who look after five cell groups, zone leaders who oversee five section leaders, and a district leader who oversees up to five zone leaders. Interestingly there are nine other churches in Korea with more than 30,000 members each. All of them have experienced rapid growth by structuring their church around the cell group ministry.

A typical cell meeting could comprise the following four elements – the 'four Ws' as they are often known...

Welcome

The group settles down, maybe with an 'icebreaker' question or game to get everyone thinking and talking, and ensuring that every group member participates right from the start, hearing their own voice out loud and feeling included.

Worship

Either sung worship or anything exalting God, such as reading from the Bible, prayer (both speaking and listening) or other creative forms of worship such as drawing and writing.

Word

This is the main 'teaching' element: applying the Bible to life, perhaps with the help of other resources such as books, DVDs or a study based on the Sunday sermon. This is also usually the time when people will minster to each other through prayer.

Witness

The aim is to see friends and neighbours come to Christ. This time is often based on planning outreach of various forms or actually acting on those plans.

G12

Forms of cell church exist throughout the world. Of particular note is the G12 system developed by pastor César Castellanos, founder of Mission Charismatic International (MCI), Bogotá, Colombia. Castellanos believed that God gave him an outline of how he could structure his church. His vision was the 'government of 12' principle, a pyramid of discipleship and authority. He suggests that because Israel had 12 tribes, and Christ had 12 disciples, the Church could base its structure on this governmental model and be made up of cell churches.

A pastor trains 12 people to be cell leaders. These cell leaders are then responsible for discipling 12 others in a cell group, usually with a minimum number coming from the community and not from within the church they attend. After a set period, and after certain strict requirements are met, these cell members then become leaders themselves, and start their own cells. Thus, the membership of the church is multiplied, and the message of the gospel is taken into the community.

Cell churches are not without their critics, with some regarding the rigidity of the approach to be legalistic. But no one can argue with their numerical success: MCI is one of the largest churches in South America, with more than 200,000 members and more than 45,000 cell groups in the city of Bogotá.

Meta church

The 'meta' model is an attempt to adjust and adapt the cell church model. It was pioneered by Carl George for a North American context. He believed that (then) current models of church ministry simply did not provide sufficient quality care to sustain a growing church. He has a broader view of what a cell might include: Sunday school classes, ministry teams, outreach teams, worship production teams, sports teams, recovery groups, and more. He says that any time 16 or fewer people meet together, you have a small group meeting.

Kings Church High Wycombe implemented a change that was similar to a meta church. They were concerned both with the attendance at small groups, and their struggle to interest anyone in leading a group. After much research and visiting churches with different models, they decided to adopt a new structure and approach for small groups. The small groups would include a classic small group focus of Bible study, fellowship and prayer. But in addition there would be a whole host of other small groups such as groups that would meet for fellowship around a shared activity where non-believers were also welcome (such as parent and toddler meetings).

Every small group would last a term, with those attending signing up for a term. If the small group continues (and many do) those attending have first chance of attending. Attendance is booked online. They found that people were prepared to lead a group knowing that they were not signing their life away, and that they would have a variety of group options.

If you want to learn more you can listen to my interview with leader Richard Lodge, found under 'The Leadership File' on iTunes.

Mid-size groups

The concept of 'mid-size groups' or 'missional communities' has been popular with some churches. Its origins in the UK are believed to be St Thomas Church, Crookes, Sheffield, a church that has a structure of mid-sized congregations (around 30 people defined as 'a community that is small enough to have a common vision, but big enough to do something about it'.). It also has 'huddles', which are around 6–12 leaders who invest in and support each other and smaller groups (led by the leaders from huddles). They believe all groups need to 'look' in three directions: upward (relationship with God), inward (relationship with each another) and outward (relationship with those outside the church). The groups are discouraged from meeting in the church, although groups with a focus on the elderly, for example, are best suited to using the church lounge. At the time of writing, groups meet in homes, cafes, bars, and even a garage, with a big emphasis on the bar and café culture in the city centre.

A missional community may focus on an area of mission and is released to do this, but remaining part of the overall wider church, with whom it meets monthly for celebrations. In more recent years, smaller teams of maybe three or four have sought to be missional together. You can find out more about mid-size groups at www.3dmovements.com

In other churches, such as Holy Trinity Brompton (home of Alpha), these mid-size groups are called 'pastorates' made up of 20–35 people. Despite its name (sounding pastoral) they get involved in 'every aspect of church life' including missional activities such as mission and social action, prayer ministry and Alpha courses.

These examples demonstrate that for some, small group ministry is a vital vehicle for church life. If there were no small groups, there would be no church. They can be a vital tool for evangelism, in training and equipping Christians, and as places where non-believers can gather to discuss issues and consider the Bible. The Alpha course, which has been attended by more than one million people in the UK, is heavily based on small group principles for the discussion part.

Which of the above, if any, is the most attractive option to you?

_____

_____

_____

_____

What difficulties do you envisage?

_____

_____

_____

_____

Managing an overhaul

Here are a few tips to approaching, implementing and developing a new approach for small groups.

You need all leaders involved to be on board

A major change requires leaders to believe it is right. Cast your vision to them, suggest why remaining the same is not the option to take, describe what the changes will lead to in the future, and give opportunity for feedback. The feedback may create opportunity for compromise and adjustment. You will need to show how things can be better for all involved. Remember that Nehemiah encouraged people to rebuild the wall close to where they were living. This had a practical dimension of course (it was closest) but suggested that the workers would be motivated to do a good job because they would be well protected because of it.

Hopefully your other leaders are keen to change, but some may already be running groups that function well. If they have invested in the members, it can be painful to envisage any adjustments. Therefore be sensitive and careful as you approach this.

You could try the 'beta level' approach

When there is resistance to an idea, it is sometimes possible to try something out in a small way first. Maybe the church leadership are not prepared to change the small groups wholesale, but would consider some new experimental groups that function in addition to the present structure.

You could suggest that these be reviewed after a year (or if they are course-based small groups, after the course). You might be wondering whether all this is worth the hassle and be secretly thinking, 'Who am I to try and change things?' The answer is that you are indwelt by the Spirt of God and are part of the body. If God is at work in and through you, there is no reason why you cannot be a catalyst to improve your small group and your church's small groups.

You need to give it time

Our excitement at a new vision can lead us to want to act tomorrow. Those listening to the ideas will need time to adjust, especially if they have bought into the way things used to be done. They would not want to feel that they are being rushed into things. Unless you have a church that has 'change' built into its DNA (and there are some like that), there will be a section of the church that will not want to change, and need the time to reflect.

Finally

I hope you have enjoyed these ten keys to small group leadership. My prayer is that this book will serve you as a valuable tool, time and time again, inspiring change and growth in the life of your group.

For more help for leading your small group, explore Small Group Central for resources, articles and tips. Visit **www.smallgroupcentral.org.uk**

If you would like to invite CWR to bring further small group training to you, visit **www.cwr.org.uk/wecancometoyou**

May God do in and through you more than you can ask or even imagine.

SmallGroup central

All of our small group ideas and resources in one place

Online:

www.smallgroupcentral.org.uk is filled with free video teaching, tools, articles and a whole host of ideas.

TRANSFORMED
LIVING

TRANSFORMED LIFE

COVER TO
cover

On the road:

A range of seminars themed for small groups can be brought to your local community. Contact us at **hello@smallgroupcentral.org.uk**

Every Day
with Jesus
extra

40
JESUS

In print:

Books, study guides and DVDs covering an extensive list of themes, Bible books and life issues.

Liz Babbs
STUDY GUIDE

Find out more at:
www.smallgroupcentral.org.uk

vital:

ToolBox

The popular *Cover to Cover* Bible study series for you or your small group

Gain a deeper understanding of God and His Word through these insightful guides, which cover more than sixty topics and Bible books. The seven stimulating sessions in each book include icebreakers, Bible verses, discussion starters, personal application and leader's notes – perfect for individual group study.

Choose your next topic or theme to study, find out current prices and order at **www.cwr.org.uk**

Available online or from Christian bookshops.

Courses and events

Waverley Abbey College

Publishing and media

Conference facilities

Transforming lives

CWR's vision is to enable people to experience personal transformation through applying God's Word to their lives and relationships.

Our Bible-based training and resources help people around the world to:
• Grow in their walk with God
• Understand and apply Scripture to their lives
• Resource themselves and their church
• Develop pastoral care and counselling skills
• Train for leadership
• Strengthen relationships, marriage and family life and much more.

Our insightful writers provide daily Bible reading notes and other resources for all ages, and our experienced course designers and presenters have gained an international reputation for excellence and effectiveness.

CWR's Training and Conference Centres in Surrey and East Sussex, England, provide excellent facilities in idyllic settings – ideal for both learning and spiritual refreshment.

CWR Applying God's Word
to everyday life and relationships

CWR, Waverley Abbey House,
Waverley Lane, Farnham,
Surrey GU9 8EP, UK

Telephone: +44 (0)1252 784700
Email: info@cwr.org.uk
Website: www.cwr.org.uk

Registered Charity No. 294387
Company Registration No. 1990308